I0706857

WHAT IF

PAMELA FULTON

authorHOUSE®

AuthorHouse™
1663 Liberty Drive
Bloomington, IN 47403
www.authorhouse.com
Phone: 833-262-8899

Published by AuthorHouse 09/25/2021

ISBN: 978-1-6655-3960-9 (sc)
ISBN: 978-1-6655-3959-3 (e)

Print information available on the last page.

Any people depicted in stock imagery provided by Getty Images are models, and such images are being used for illustrative purposes only.
Certain stock imagery © Getty Images.

This book is printed on acid-free paper.

1

What if we were never divided by color or race?

a. The world would be different
b. There would be more love and less hatred in the world

2

What if slavery never existed?

a. There would be less problems in the world today
b. The world would be worse off

3

What if we never had people like Martin Luther King?

a. African-Americans would still be slaves today
b. All Americans would be free

4

What if we never had abusive marriages?

a. Marriages would last longer
b. Marriages would be worse off

5

What if we've never been rape victims?

a. There would be a more peaceful world today
b. There would be a less peaceful world today

6

What if we never abandoned our children?

a. There would be more students academically achieving in the U.S.
b. There would be less students academically achieving in the U.S.

7

What if guns were never invented?

a. There would be less deaths in the world
b. There would be more deaths in the world

8

What if no one ever had to starve?

a. There would be less deaths
b. There would be more deaths

9

What if everything was free?

a. There would be less stress in the world
b. There would be more stress and stealing

10

What if there was no animal abuse?

a. Animals would be happier
b. Animals would be more friendly

11

What if we never had policemen?

a. There would be less deaths for African-Americans.
b. There would be more deaths for African-Americans.

12

What if we never had the army or any other soldiers?

a. Soldiers who lost lives in war would have lived longer

b. No one would fight for our country

13

What if bombs were never made?

a. Lives that ended by bombs may have lasted longer
b. The world would be a better place

14

What if drugs were never invented?

a. The world would be worse off
b. The world would be better off

15

What if alcohol never existed?

a. The world would be better off
b. The world would be worse off

16

What if death didn't exist?

a. Everyone will be less stressed
b. Everyone will be more stressed

17

What if no one ever had a reason to be sad?

a. We would have peace on Earth
b. There would be no peace on Earth

18

What if we never grew old?

a. We would stay young forever
b. We would lose all of our hair

19

What if mental abuse never occurred?

a. There would be a happier world
b. There would be more depression

20

What if men had babies instead of women?

a. Men would appreciate women more
b. Men will respect women more

21

What if we all felt free and equal?

a. There would be peace on Earth
b. Justice would be served

22

What if we all loved one another?

a. We would have peace
b. We would have freedom

23

What if there was no killing?

a. The world would be peaceful
b. The world would be awful

24

What if there was no stealing?

a. There would be less people in jail
b. There would be more people in jail

25

What if we could leave everything unlocked and still feel safe?

a. We would get robbed
b. People in the world would trust others more and everyone on Earth would be one big family

26

What if we can all breathe?

a. All rights would be equal
b. All would be treated as one

27

What if everyone believed in God and lived by his words?

a. There would be peace on Earth
b. Everyone would go to heaven and live forever

28

What if school bullying ended?

a. Students would feel less stressed and anxious while in school
b. Students would feel more free to express themselves and their ideas

29

What if everyone in the world needing assistance with their mental health got the help they needed?

a. Everyone in the world would be more at ease
b. Everyone in the world would fight each other

30

What if we all finally had peace and a happily ever after?

a. We would all feel united
b. The world would be more chaotic

ANSWERS

1. **A and B**	16. A
2. **A**	17. A
3. **A**	18. A
4. **A**	19. A
5. **A**	20. **A and B**
6. **A**	21. **A and B**
7. **A**	22. **A and B**
8. **A**	23. A
9. **A**	24. A
10. **A and B**	25. **B**
11. A	26. **A and B**
12. **A and B**	27. **A and B**
13. **A and B**	28. **A and B**
14. **B**	29. A
15. A	30. A

ABOUT THE AUTHOR

Pamela Fulton lives in Iowa but is from Chicago, Illinois. She was born in 1973. She has 4 children (Eddie, Khalil, Shawn, and Kwan) and is married to Shawn. Also, she has a dog named Tank.